Followship

The *Essence* of Our Journey with Jesus

JERRY GILLIS

TATE PUBLISHING, LLC

Acknowledgements

All of the following people have shared in helping make this book a reality. I would like to say thanks. . .

To Edie, Trace and Tanner—I could not love you more.

To my Dad, who genetically passed to me the "urge to write."

To my Mom, who has always been my cheerleader.

To Steve and Renee, and Suzanne and Carter–thanks for the solid foundation of friendship and the feeling that I am always at home with you.

My extended family–you have been, in various ways, a source of encouragement, instruction and inspiration at many points along the journey. Thank you.

To the wonderful people and staff of The Chapel–thank you for letting me be free to learn to follow the One who is the Head of the Church. God graced me with you.

To the publishing family at Tate–thanks for taking a chance on a first-time author. I am appreciative of the hard work and help in birthing this project.

To the various people who have shaped me in ministry–Johnny Hunt, John Cross, Jim Law, Dan Dorner, Al Cockrell, and a host of others–I am indebted to you for your investment and belief in me, and for modeling the desire to be followers first.

To Kemper–thanks for helping me see this book clearly.

To Kay–thank you for showing me where and how the journey begins.

To the untold, and often unheralded, millions that have followed Jesus before me. I look forward to the day where the complete Fellowship of Followers will be gathered with the Great Leader for the New Beginning.

Contents

Foreword

I was pleased when Jerry first informed me that he was writing a book on the subject of followship. I was especially delighted when he asked me to write the foreword. Jerry Gillis, for many reasons, qualifies for the writing of this book, not the least of these is the manner in which he has conducted himself in his relatively brief ministry life. He is not only my friend, he is my colleague. Together we serve a wonderful church known as The Chapel. Unlike many co-pastor relationships, our relationship is a true partnership in every sense of the word. Often a co-pastor is more of a "junior co-pastor" or what we often refer to as an associate pastor. From the outset of our relationship I had as one of my ministry objectives to position this ministry for aggressive ministry effectiveness with a target on the future.

In order for this plan to be successful I had to find a leader who knew how to follow. I found that man in Jerry Gillis. He was an effective leader in his own right but had the wisdom at a very young age to realize that leadership and experience are two different things. When we first embarked on this journey of sharing ministry he was the ripe old age of 32, young by ministry standards. The special quality that has played an important part in making this relationship work is his willingness to assume certain roles of leadership without clamoring for more. He easily moved from leading to following depending on what his specific responsibility happened to be.

When he speaks of priority, one of the chapter

titles of "Followship," he is not merely speaking theory. He effectively communicates that if one is to have as his priority following Jesus it must encompass the whole of the person. I have watched as Jerry becomes what I believe will be a great leader and pastor, and I see his devotion to the One that saved him some fifteen years ago as unswerving.

When he discusses the subject of advance it becomes clear that the only true progress one makes in life is limited to the times that we have made Jesus the priority and without reservation have wholeheartedly followed Him. Authenticity, mission, trust, and courage are either demonstrated or fulfilled by one's willingness to follow Him.

God does a remarkable thing by placing us in unique human relationships. Those relationships become the grid of how well we play out the reality or lack of it as it relates to followship. The relationship that God has ordained for Jerry and I has placed him in a position where he must be a good leader simply because of the thousands of people that he is responsible for. He must be a good follower because all of those people must have an example of what a good follower looks like.

As you journey through the pages of this book it will become evident that out of this young mind a deep, age-old, abiding truth has emerged. That truth is the fresh growth of a new adventure–a church united around the priority of following Jesus.

Al Cockrell
Senior Co-Pastor
The Chapel
February, 2005

Introduction

Follow Me. These two words of Jesus strike an unbelievably deep yet very simple chord. They were spoken over 2,000 years ago on the rocky shore of the Sea of Galilee, and the waves have carried the echo for two millennia. It seems somewhat awkward that Jesus made His grand call so simple. *Follow me?* Shouldn't the Son of God, the Messiah, have a much more complex and detailed way of inviting us to share His life? A lightning bolt that split the Sea of Galilee and carved the names of those receiving this incredible invitation on the ocean floor would have seemed appropriate, or perhaps Jesus speaking in a divinely cryptic language that could only be heard through special decoder seashells found by the most intelligent and innovative of the bunch—anything. Just make it harder and more complex, you know, more suitable to Godness. But it was not complex. His words were simple and personal. In the language of Jesus' day, his comment could more directly be understood to mean, *[You] follow me.* Incredibly simple. Deeply personal. Highly mysterious. For me, the mystery of this phrase has been primarily found in the first word - Follow. Growing up in an age of technological advance and innovation, I assumed that the most notable thing one could aspire to was leadership. Lead a company. Lead the money list on the PGA. Lead the country. Lead somebody, or for that matter, lead anybody. It seemed a matter of incontrovertible truth that leaders were good, and followers were destined for trouble. Maybe that is why it seemed troubling to me that Jesus wanted me to be a follower.

Before I get too far ahead of myself, let me make it clear that I don't think that leadership is bad. Quite the contrary. The Bible is replete with examples of excellent leaders from both the Old and New Testaments. Moses, Joshua, Gideon, David, Esther, Paul, James, and Timothy are just a sample. But I think their excellence in leadership was only as great as their ability to follow God. They were, first and foremost, followers.

Maybe Jesus asks us to follow Him to make a rather stark point: There is already a Leader. No need for you or me to try and take the reigns of leadership. Jesus has everything covered. He will let us know if He needs any help leading everyone and everything (don't hold your breath). I recognize that this seems simplistic, but we often miss it. We act, at times, as if we are the last person left on the planet who has the capacity to govern the planet. We behave as if everything hinges on our decision-making and organizational leadership skills. We take our abilities, and our very selves, far too seriously. And we ultimately lose ourselves in the process, all for the sake of the attainment of leadership.

The lure of leadership is strong. By that, I don't mean to imply that it is bad. Like anything else it can certainly be abused, but leadership is not inherently wrong. It becomes troublesome for us when it promises those things that scratch us where we itch. We take the bait and swallow what is on the hook. Prestige. Recognition. Power. But upon attaining those things, we find ourselves categorized with the untold, unsatisfied millions through the ages who form the "fellowship of the duped." Leadership, as an end in itself, simply does not satisfy us at the core of our being.

Many are pulled to leadership for the wrong reasons, but others are drawn to it for other, more rational, reasons. For example, life seems too short to embrace a vanilla existence, so leadership gives one the ability to really live and feel. It creates a sense of adventure–a pioneering spirit. Many want to lead simply because the alternative feels like no life at all. This rationale doesn't really trouble me; that is, until it makes its way into the Jesus arena. Some have wrongly assumed that living life taking orders from someone else, anyone else, would be no life at all. They consider themselves to be free people, and they intend to keep it that way. But our freedom can end up being our bondage because we find ourselves successful yet not significant, and powerful yet discontented. Look around. Sports stars. Hollywood celebrities. CEOs. Pastors. Soccer moms. Nobody is immune from this dreaded disease.

But there is hope, a vaccination, if you will. Live life as a follower. Following helps us. As upside down as it sounds, it frees us. It takes us out of the bondage of our own selfishness and vanity and places us in an arena that is outside of ourselves. It is full of adventure and wonder and discovery because we are not at the controls and don't know what each new turn will bring. We really live when we follow, and it is a noble life. Followers live for the prestige, recognition, and glory of Another. Life is no longer centered on self. And the less focused that we are on self, the more we seem to help ourselves at the core of our being.

Of course, this is no surprise to The Leader, Jesus. He wasn't trying to squelch our independence or giftedness when He called us to follow Him. He was enhancing it. He wasn't trying to be dictatorial in a tyrannical sense when He called us. He was inviting us to share a life with Him and live in a mutual relationship. He wasn't taking away our lives by calling us to follow. He was showing

11

us how to truly live. This Leader is worth living for and dying for as well.

While following is noble, it is not always easy. It is rewarding, in part, because it is so challenging. What you will find in the following chapters is a brief look at some of what it takes to be a follower of Jesus. You will notice that some of these same characteristics could be required for leaders as well. But there is one major difference: Following comes first, leading comes later. Jesus didn't ask to be led; He desired to be followed. For those that are serious about joining the fellowship of followers, the journey has to have a beginning. That beginning is your willingness to surrender the reigns of your life to the Leader, Jesus. My prayer is that as you read the following chapters through the eyes of a surrendered follower, The Leader will show you a journey rich with wonder and profound in its influence upon others.

Chapter I

Priority

I can remember it like it was yesterday. My wife and I, along with our oldest son, had made our way to the mall. My wife was there because she loves the mall. I was there because I love my wife. Since I am admittedly not a fan of walking aimlessly through a sea of stores to determine whether or not I could save four cents on a three dollar product, I look for things to do to occupy my time. Of course, I usually only do them in my mind because my wife likes for me to look like I am part of the whole shopping experience. No mind games on this day though. This was the real deal. You see, my son, who was two at the time, decided to take a stroll on his own. Most kids at this age have some mysterious, invisible leash that begins to tighten if the child gets more than about thirty feet away from the parent. Not mine. He could take off at any minute and not think twice about it. I would always worry that if I didn't pay close enough attention, he would walk right out of the store, hail a taxi, and end up marching down Main Street U.S.A. alongside the seven dwarfs at Disney World without ever giving us a second thought.

Fortunately, I was paying attention on this day when my son decided to embark on his journey of exploration. He left the store we were in and started walking down the mall just taking in all of the sights. At a safe distance, I carefully followed him. He never turned around; he just kept walking - into and out of stores, back and forth, up and down aisles. Suddenly, it started to get complicated for me because I had to work at keeping up with him. First, the lady at the perfume counter wanted to stop me and give me some samples, but without taking my eyes off of my son I said, "No thanks." Then, as he came out of another store, I had to avoid the dreaded mall questionnaire people so that I could keep up with him. My little boy had no idea where he was going, and the truth is he didn't care. But I did. This was my son. I had to stay with him. Everything and everyone else in those few minutes was secondary because I had only one priority—following my son.

As a Christ follower, we must understand that following requires priority. But, unlike the example with my son, the One we are following knows where He is going, and we are the ones who will find ourselves disoriented if we don't keep up. Anyone and anything else is secondary to Jesus. Now, this does not mean that Jesus doesn't allow us to have relationships, or jobs, or leisure. It simply means that all of these things are secondary to our relationship with the Leader that we follow. This will be tested in your life. There will be many people on your spiritual journey trying to give you perfume samples and coaxing you into filling out questionnaires, but you and I cannot become sidetracked or lose sight of the One we follow. Following requires priority, and we can only give Jesus our highest priority when we give Him our highest love. Whomever or whatever we love the most always gets our highest priority. For Romeo it was Juliet. For Gollum it was The Ring. And for the brave hearted William Wallace, it was freedom for his people.

But as the follower of Christ, our priority must never be another person, or a possession, or even some abstract cause. Our priority must always be Jesus.

To make sure that we are clear on the use of the term priority, let's take a look at the word as defined by the American Heritage Dictionary of English Language:

Priority - from Latin word *prior*

1) Precedence, especially established by order of importance or urgency

2) a. An established right to precedence

   b. An authoritative rating that established such precedence

3) A preceding or coming earlier in time

4) Something afforded or deserving of prior attention

With that definition in view, we can observe three arenas of our lives where our following of Jesus must be given precedence.

Priority in Relationships

When Jesus explained to his followers what their allegiances, or priorities, were to look like, He didn't sugar coat it. In fact, through some difficult language to digest, He cut right to the heart of allegiances and talked about the issue of relationships.

He who loves father or mother more than Me

*is not worthy of Me. And he who loves son or
daughter more than Me is not worthy of Me.*
Matthew 10:37

In another passage of Scripture, Jesus said,

*If anyone comes to Me and does not hate his
father and mother, wife and children, brothers
and sisters, yes, and his own life also, he cannot be My disciple.*
Luke 14:26

I can see your faces as you read these passages of
Scripture - the crumpled brow, the questioning look, the
eyes rolling in the back of your head. "Surely you can't
be telling me that Jesus wants us to hate the other relationships in our lives." Of course not (and don't call me
Shirley). When the Bible uses terms to describe emotions
or affections, they are often comparative terms. In other
words, Jesus is saying that the allegiance that He desires
from his followers, when compared to other relationship
allegiances, would be so starkly different that it would
appear to be hate. Love for Jesus must be such a priority, so superior in importance, that the follower's relationship to Him trumps every other possible relationship. The
level of disdain for other relationships is not what is in
view here; instead, it is the grandness of love for Jesus
that is the point.

Listen, Jesus doesn't want you to hate your mom
and dad, or wife, or siblings or children. He wants you to
love them well. But the best way to love anyone well is
to be properly related to the well of love and to have your
priority affections and allegiances set on Him. Simply
stated, when your love relationship to Jesus is in proper

priority, you will love those around you in a way that reminds them of Jesus.

Another thing needs to be very clear though. Jesus desires nothing short of top billing, highest priority, numero uno in importance, and He is allowed to make that claim. If anyone else in your life made that claim, it would be from arrogance or self-absorption or a burning need for affirmation. But not Jesus. You see, as part of the triune Godhead (Father, Son, and Holy Spirit - three in one), He has the right to make any claim He wants. It is not a claim of arrogance; its just fact. As designer, author, architect and navigator of your life, His credentials speak for themselves. And as your sinless substitute, the One who paid the price for your sin debt to appease the justice of God, He is not out of line to ask for that kind of allegiance. He made it crystal clear that if our priority relationship was not Him, that we would not be worthy to be His followers. Every relationship hinges on, and actually pales in comparison to, the priority of our relationship to Jesus.

This truth is often easily eroded in the context of our day-to-day relationships. You can see it in the beautiful young college girl that loses her mind over the "perfect" guy, even though it is clear that he is not a follower of Jesus. Her desire to change him along with thoughts that maybe one day he will "come around" are just futile efforts to hide the truth that Jesus' priority has vanished. And what about the man in his mid-forties who takes his eyes off Jesus and looks closer and closer into the mirror next to him and sees the need to trade in his aging wife for a newer model? Or the retired couple that decides that this newfound freedom is "our time," and they check out of service to the Lord and out of passionately following Jesus? Relationships can quickly become sinking ships when the priority allegiance is not properly focused because we are designed by God to live in relationship to Him. When that relationship becomes secondary, then so does our spiritual sanity.

Priority over our Occupation

The precedence of Jesus is not just related to our relationships, but is in truth related to everything we are. This includes our jobs. Western civilization has a convenient tendency to compartmentalize life in such a way that we have a home life, a work life, a recreational life, a spiritual life, and so on. For the follower of Jesus, however, there are no compartments. His call to follow is holistic.

This can be seen in full color through the life of some of Jesus' earliest followers. If you could interview one of them, Matthew (some of his buddies called him Levi), you would see the impact of His call. The Bible records it this way,

> *As Jesus passed on from there, He saw a man named Matthew sitting at the tax office. And He said to him, "Follow Me." So he arose and followed Him.*
> *Matthew 9:9*

Seems easy enough when we read it. The problem begins when we start to digest it. Matthew was making a pretty healthy income albeit from some unethical means. The tax collectors of Jesus' day were looked upon in the same way as some personal injury lawyers or televangelists or psychic friends' network employees may be looked upon in our day. They were neither liked nor trusted. First, they suffered the natural dislike aimed at people whose job it is to take your hard earned money. Second, because of their job, these tax collectors interacted with Gentiles. As a result, the Jews would look at them as ceremonially unclean. Finally, and probably the strongest in generating disgust, the tax collectors were operatives for the oppressive Romans and thus viewed as traitors to their country, Israel.

So, there sits Matthew one day just doing his job, collecting the taxes. And along comes a Jew that was thought of as a rabbi by most, a holy man. And the holy man tells the hated, disreputable sinner/tax collector to leave behind his work and follow Him. That part, as strange as it seems, I can live with. It's the next part that troubles me. Matthew actually does it. I mean, what was he thinking? Did it ever occur to him that everyone else hated the only friends he had, and the only job he had now branded him with a reputation that he could never live down? If that did dawn on him, then what possessed him to shut off the message in his brain that said it would be a disaster to give up your income, leave the only people that like you, and hang out with a holy man and some other Jews (who will most likely hate you too)?

To be honest, I don't really know. Now, I realize in a theological realm that it was the design of God for this to happen. What I can't process is what it must have been like for Matthew to actually do it. Upon leaving that job, he had to know that if things with the holy man didn't work out, that no self-respecting Jew would ever hire him for a decent job again. And how do you make friends with people that already don't like you before you ever meet them?

I admire Matthew. Sure, I could have talked about

Peter and Andrew leaving their boats and following Jesus. Or even James and John. They left their livelihoods to follow Jesus too didn't they? Of course. But what stands out to me is that in leaving everything behind, Peter still had his brother Andrew. James still had his brother John. And Matthew? Well, Matthew had, um, Matthew. That's what I admire. He left his occupation and demonstrated the priority of following Jesus, and he did it alone. Matthew had "guts," you know, good old-fashioned intestinal fortitude. The truth is it takes a little bit of guts to allow Jesus to be the priority over your occupation because it may mean that He asks you leave it to follow Him somewhere else.

So what does this mean for us? That's a great question. I guess it means it really is true that we can't allow Jesus to have priority in some areas but not in all of them. He is the priority in everything, yes, even our jobs. The great news in all of this is that if Jesus asks us to leave our occupation for His sake, He is not asking just to try and break us down. Again, let's take Matthew for example. Instead of being despised and rejected by the holy man, Jesus shows up at Matthew's house for a party. The guests of the party aren't tea and crumpets people. They are more like whiskey sour people. Yet Jesus uses Matthew as a bridge to walk into their lives and bring a message of hope and forgiveness. Then Matthew develops friendships with some other men in Jesus' entourage who quickly become a band of brothers that look past their old ways of life and are united around the priority of following Jesus. Who would have thought that Matthew would ever have this life, this impact? Certainly not Matthew. And I don't know if Matthew was a singer or not (if he was, most of the songs he knew probably weren't tunes that he could sing in the synagogue), but had the

hymn been written in Matthew's time, I imagine that its significance to Matthew would have been real:
"Though none go with me, I still will follow."

And to think Matthew's journey started with giving Jesus higher importance than his occupation. What do you think might happen if we allowed Jesus to have the higher importance over our jobs? Might He use us more effectively in our places of employment? Certainly. Might He ask us to leave and follow Him somewhere else that He leads? Possibly. But, rest assured, whatever He asks you to do will be worth it, even if He asks you to do it alone.

Priority over Ourselves

The Christmas season is one of my favorite times of the year. In truth, now that I am in Buffalo, it is getting even better because I can be nearly positive that it will snow on Christmas—of course, the chances aren't much less that it will snow on the fourth of July too. When I spent eight years in south Florida, the season just was not the same. I mean, Santa in shorts and flip-flops is just the wrong mental picture.

Anyway, at Christmas a few years ago, my family and I were gathered in Atlanta with other family members to celebrate together. Christmas evening we congregated at my grandparent's house for our annual present exchange. My cousin, who was about eight or nine years old at the time, was helping pass out the presents to the other family members. After some time of present passing, he noticed that he did not have near the amount of presents everyone else had. In addition, he watched as others began opening their presents with great excitement. So, he did what any self-respecting young boy would do - he chanted. It rang out all through the room for all of us to hear, "What about me? What about me? What about me?"

While I don't make it a habit to chant very often, I feel certain that we have all sung the "What about me?" song many times. Life is great until it starts messing with me. If you don't get any presents, it's your problem. If I don't get any presents, it's everyone's problem. Ever been there?

I think we all have been there. Really, we spend more time "there" than anywhere else. We are a "me" people. We have a clear priority of ourselves first, everyone and everything else next. Now, we will make every effort to say the right things and do just enough acts of selfless service to appear that we are not all about ourselves. But we all know the truth. We are on a pursuit, and we don't think of this pursuit as selfish, we just think of it as a birthright. I mean, we are Americans, and the Declaration of Independence does provide for us the right to pursue happiness.

But Jesus is not American, and He didn't sign the Declaration of Independence. We forget that sometimes. We forget that the story of Jesus begins, as Ray Bakke noted, with an Asian born baby that became an African refugee.[1] We Westernize Jesus. He is the blue eyed, lily-white man with a British accent that the cinema portrays. And we don't just westernize His appearance; we also do it with our expectations of Him. He wants us to be rich, of course, since Americans have always placed value upon hard work, free enterprise, and the spirit of entrepreneurship. He wants us to be comfortable. He wants the majority to rule since democracy is our way of life. He wants us to be independent. He wants us to be happy.

Actually, He wants us to follow Him. And following Him means that He desires our holiness more than our happiness, our willingness to die for Him rather than live for ourselves.

> *When He had called the people to Himself, with His disciples also, He said to them, "Whoever desires to come after Me, let him deny himself, and take up his cross, and follow Me. For whoever desires to save his life will lose it, but whoever loses his life for My sake and the gospel's will save it."*
> *Mark 8:34–35*

Let's not misunderstand for a minute what the disciples were hearing and understanding Jesus to say. They knew all too well what a cross was. They passed by them more than once as the Romans made examples of Jewish revolutionaries. They knew that the cross was an instrument of death, and for Jesus to tell them that they would need a cross to follow Him, must have sent tremors through them. It would be the equivalent of Jesus showing up at your house today and telling you to follow Him, and, oh by the way, you will need to bring your own electric chair. He is making it crystal clear that his followers must turn in their priority over their own lives. Give up their rights. Shift their allegiance. Prepare to die.

For the American mind, this is especially hard to swallow. If we could peel back our western picture of Jesus for just a moment and look at Him clearly, we would see that He is not American. He's not British. He's not Canadian. And really, He is not just a Jew from Israel. He is God the Son. And His Godness is not reserved for a few Jews and even fewer Gentiles in the ancient Middle

East. He is the God of now, just like He is the God of then, and just as He is the God of later.

Our definition of priority earlier in the chapter noted something interesting. One of the facets of that definition was that priority included "a preceding or coming earlier in time." A pretty obvious reason that Jesus deserves priority over our own lives is that He made us. He came "earlier in time" so to speak. We exist because of Him, and our only real existence will continue through Him. If we try to manage our own lives, navigate our own course, we will end in futility. As Jesus said, *"For whoever desires to save his life will lose it, but whoever loses his life for My sake and the gospel's will save it."* The truth of this statement is that dying to ourselves is really living. Jim Eliot, missionary to the Auca Indians of Ecuador, summed up these statements of Jesus in brilliant fashion when he said, "He is no fool who gives what he cannot keep, to gain what he cannot lose."[2] Jim Eliot obviously believed that statement because shortly after writing it, he was killed by those same Indians to whom he was preaching the message of life in Jesus. But I imagine that if he could talk to us today, he would make sure that we knew he didn't lose anything in giving his life for Jesus. He traded his priorities for the priority of following Jesus long before that.

Chapter II

Advance

Now when He got into a boat,
His disciples followed Him.
Matthew 8:23

At the risk of seeming trivial and highly unintelligent at the same time, I think it is important that I highlight a critical facet of following. To follow means you must actually go somewhere. I know it seems as if I am re-stating the obvious, but I think there is some merit to exploring it. Following implies movement, activity. Maybe even better stated, it implies advance. You can't follow by standing still. You have to keep up with the one being followed. That is why when Jesus got into a boat, His disciples piled in with Him. They knew He was headed somewhere, advancing, so they had to do the same.

In the books and articles of the emerging church, the term of choice for describing our Christian experience is that of a *journey*. I don't think that term is just a cozy metaphor for a generation that has rejected the vocabulary of their predecessors. I think it is accurate. My reasoning for this is tied up in the meaning of the word "follow." In the original language of the New Testament, the word for *follow* has as its root the word for *road*. In other words, the word *follow* was originally understood to mean that you join someone who precedes you on the road. You journey with him, but he is the clear leader since you are the follower. You advance with the Leader on your journey.

Every epic of antiquity always had the principal character advancing in some way on his journey. Odysseus in Homer's *Odyssey*, Aeneas in Virgil's *Aeneid*, and even Gulliver in Jonathan Swift's *Gulliver's Travels* were all on the move in their respective journeys. Noticeably absent in the various epics of old are the main characters standing still or staying put. Of course, they were at times forcibly retained, held captive, and otherwise encumbered on their journeys, but usually at first opportunity they were back on the road heading for their final destinations. The epic would probably not have been of such force had the lead characters not been people of advance. I just can't imagine Homer writing six hundred pages about the long boring days of Odysseus surrounded by the same scenery in the same city with the same people. That is not an epic. It would be more like a nap. What makes the epic an epic is that there is adventure and discovery and advance.

This concept of advance was made clearer to me recently on a family excursion to an apple farm. This place was in the middle of nowhere. New York is a big state with a lot of farmland, particularly in the central portion of the state, and I thought that on our way to the farm, we saw all of it. As we were driving there, I was convinced that even if we had a global positioning system in our car, it would have said, "You are on your own." But we finally made it, and it turned out that the place was actually pretty cool. There were animals to pet, slides, pedal cars, apple pies, clowns, more apple pies, and this cornfield maze. I enjoyed the whole experience, but what

I really wanted to do was to go into that cornfield maze. At first, the maze experience was a little weird because I was having some childhood flashbacks that I was going to be some stooge in a *Children of the Corn* sequel, and some red haired, freckle faced dude was going to walk out with a sickle and mess me up. After seeing the courage of my two young boys, however, I got over my cowardice relatively quickly.

Not more than one minute into the maze, our children took off with some friends' children and started running as fast as they could. After they had plenty of time to escape, I began running after them just for the fun of playing in the maze. I would catch them sometimes, then they would run off and we would start the process all over again. After catching them a final time, we let them know that it was time to go. So, as all good children would do, they took off again. As I made my way around the maze trying to figure out how to exit, I finally just stopped and tried to think. After standing there for a little bit, two boys that were not my own came up to me and asked me, "How do you get out of here?"

Looking somewhat reflective for a minute (which is what adults do when they don't know the answer but still want to look wise), it finally dawned on me. "Well boys, we can't get out of a maze by standing still, can we?" So we took off, made a few wrong turns, but eventually got out. I had successfully led these boys to safety and was feeling rather heroic until I looked up and saw my wife had made it out before me, so had our friends and our kids (one of which is three). I didn't want to play anymore.

You can't get out of a maze by standing still. Think all you want, but you must advance at some point to actually get out. I think, in some sense, we have forgotten that in our journey, our epic, we are to be people of advance. Mental assent is not enough. We must actually do something. This is true in the process of beginning our journey as a Jesus follower. We can't just acknowledge that we need to take a journey. We can't just agree that following Jesus is the right thing to do. We must actually do it. Even though our mind is involved, salvation is not only in our minds, but in our hearts as well—and our feet. The epic does not begin until we hit the road and follow the Leader.

The apostle Paul is a good example of a follower who advanced through the maze of his journey. In an often overlooked passage that chronicles a portion of Paul's journey, we read:

> *Now when they had gone through Phrygia and the region of Galatia, they were forbidden by the Holy Spirit to preach the word in Asia. After they had come to Mysia, they tried to go into Bithynia, but the Spirit did not permit them. So passing by Mysia, they came down to Troas. And a vision appeared to Paul in the night. A man of Macedonia stood and pleaded with him, saying, "Come over to Macedonia and help us." Now after he had seen the vision, immediately we sought to go to Macedonia, concluding that the Lord had called us to preach the gospel to them.*
> *Acts 16:6–10*

The Holy Spirit stopped Paul from advancing in one direction, so he decided to advance in another, and another. Paul, whose primary motivation in life was to get the good news of Jesus to all the people that he could, was actually not permitted to go to some places to share his message. Why? I would not want to speculate since only God really knows, but that is not the point of this scene. What is interesting is that Paul never stopped advancing even when God held him up in going one direction. He just simply went another direction. If you were to consult a map that was representative of the time of Paul's journey, and then cross reference this passage with that map, you would find that Paul was virtually prohibited from going north, south, or east. The only option left was a relatively western direction. The problem of going west, however, was that Paul would run into the Mediterranean Sea eventually. At last check, the evangelistic responses of sea urchins were not very promising. So, there is Paul lying on the beach at Troas (or maybe he is not on the beach, but work with me here), and he must have been thinking that all he wanted to do was to tell people about the great Savior, Jesus. And then it happened. God sent a vision to Paul that the people of Macedonia, who were located on a beach across the Mediterranean, needed him. Paul answered this Macedonian call and had the impact of an earthquake in Philippi, Thessalonica, and Berea. And how did he end up there? He advanced.

For a follower the rule is to advance. The exception is to stand still. And on occasion, the Lord will ask you to stop and be still (Exodus 14:13, Job 37:14, Psalm 46:10). But you can't get out of a maze by just standing around. And Paul didn't stand around. He completely trusted in the leadership and guidance of God's Spirit in his process of advance. When God didn't allow Him to go to one location, He went somewhere else. His motives were pure. His passion was fixed on Jesus. He trusted God's guidance, and he didn't stand still. He was a great picture of what God promises to those who trust Him completely as they advance:

> *Trust in the Lord with all your heart, And lean not on your own understanding; In all your ways acknowledge Him, And He shall direct your paths.*
> *Proverbs 3:5–6*

Paul knew that his responsibility was to trust the One he followed in every way. He also knew that it was Jesus' responsibility to direct him. The truth about direction is that it implies we are already moving, advancing. And when we advance with a heart that has complete allegiance to Jesus, we can trust that Jesus will make sure we are on the right path. Why wouldn't He? He is the One who has called us to follow. He's not playing hide and seek; He is asking us to follow the Leader.

I'm convinced that another reason that advance is so important and implicit in the life of a Jesus follower is because faith is forward. Faith is being sure of what we hope for and certain of what we do not see (Hebrews 11:1). It points us forward, not backwards.

"But Jerry, have you forgotten about our faith in the finished work of Christ on the cross? That is obviously not forward."

I can only agree with that in part. Let me explain. Like you, I am intensely grateful for the unfathomable work of grace that occurred on our behalf through Jesus' sacrifice on the cross. It was the greatest demonstration of love ever imagined; in fact, it is an incomparable act that actually cannot be imagined by our finite minds. But it didn't end there. Jesus is not on the cross anymore. As we are reminded through the pages of the Bible, *And if Christ is not risen, your faith is futile; you are still in your sins!* (1 Corinthians 15:17). Since Christ is risen, that means that He is not just nostalgia but is a present and future tense living God. The finished work of Jesus on the cross gave humanity the opportunity to experience a relationship with God that would be impossible otherwise. And the resurrection points to the unfinished work of Jesus in heaven that guides the follower through a life designed to bring Him glory and fulfill His purposes. That is why I feel like faith is forward. It's living and active, and our faith in the living Jesus allows us the opportunity to advance with His guidance.

With this thought, I am not advocating that we try to erase all memories of our heritage, or that we purge our minds of the great works of God in the past. That would be foolish and unprofitable. What I am suggesting is that remembering and looking back are not necessarily the same things. Jesus illustrates this point after running into someone on His journey that tells Him he will follow Him after he first goes and tells his family goodbye. Notice Jesus' response,

> *"No one, having put his hand to the plow, and looking back, is fit for the kingdom of God."*
> Luke 9:62

We can't advance if we live life looking back. Because our faith is forward, and is fixed on the living Jesus, we are to advance with a heart that does not long to look back. Remember? Yes. Look back? No. You can remember without looking back because remembering is a mind position, but looking back is an eye position.

Allow me an elementary illustration. Why is

there all the traffic congestion on the highway when the vehicles in the accident have been moved off to the side? Because of "rubber-neckers," those people who just have to keep looking back at the cars well after they have passed them. In some cases, there are further reports of accidents because those looking back end up having accidents themselves. They did not see or have the ability to anticipate what was coming because the position of their eyes was looking back. In effect, it could be said that those who look back like this are potentially sabotaging their future. Remembering, however, does not put you in that position. You can remember the accident as you pass it, yet continue to advance and have the ability to deal with what is ahead. In fact, your remembrance of what occurred may actually benefit your future driving skill. Many times in the Scriptures, God instructs people to remember; yet Jesus says not to look back. Is there a communication problem in the Trinity? Obviously not. What we learn from this is remembering and looking back are not the same things. Check this out to see it more clearly:

"Remember Lot's wife."

These are the words of Jesus in Luke 17:32. What did Lot's wife do anyway that we are supposed to remember? She looked back. Mr. and Mrs. Lot lived in a town called Sodom. God was not very impressed with what the people of this town had become, so he sent two angels to let Lot know that the place was going to go up in smoke and he had better get himself and his family out of there. (To prove the point even further, the men of Sodom actually asked for the angels to have sex with them.) The angels really only gave Lot and his family one very specific, non-negotiable request. Don't look back. Whatever you do, don't look back. So they left Sodom and didn't look back, all except Lot's wife. She looked back and became a pillar of salt. And thousands of years later, Jesus says, "Remember, don't look back." Remembering and looking back are not the same. Remembering can keep us from harm and allow us to navigate the future, but looking back brings us harm and sacrifices our future.

Pastor and author, Erwin Raphael McManus, speaks about how the church for too long has been led by nostalgics instead of advancers.[3] I think he is right. We have lived and led looking backwards instead of embracing the future that the Living Jesus, the God of the now, has for us. If we live life looking backwards, it is for the purpose of perpetuating ourselves. If we lead looking backwards, it is for the purpose of perpetuating our institutions. In either case, it goes against the design God has for our lives and our leadership. Jesus did not call us to be self-perpetuators. He called us to deny ourselves, take up our cross, and follow Him. And, contrary to some popular understanding, Jesus didn't call us to perpetuate our church institutions. The institutional church (as distinguished from the body of Christ) is a vehicle to extend the kingdom of God. It is not to be self-propelling; it is to be kingdom propelling. To lead these church institutions by looking back defeats the nobler purpose because it only advances the institution. But to lead these institutions with a forward faith will advance the kingdom. And that is what we are to be about - kingdom advancement. To deny this and lead looking backwards is to imply that Jesus died for institutions or to give us a full time, salaried job in vocational ministry. But Jesus didn't die for institutions or to give you and me a job; He died for people that desperately need Him. That is why we can ill afford to look back. We must remember to advance.

One of the great killers of advance is the sin of comparison. You can see it everywhere, people constantly comparing themselves to other people, churches comparing themselves to other churches, and companies comparing themselves to other companies. At a recent conference I attended, I had the pleasure of hearing from Jim Collins, author of *Built to Last* and *Good to Great*. These books were the culmination of years of researching companies that had sustained success over the long haul and the reasons for those successes. Then, the follow up research had to do with how some companies sustained greatness while other companies with the same resources, similar products, and comparable markets, just remained good companies. After the presentation, Mr. Collins was answering questions, and he made an interesting observation. He noted that the great companies did not compare themselves to anyone; they simply had their own standard of greatness. The other companies that were in the study group, however, compared themselves to everyone else in their market.

Comparison inhibits your advance as a company. It inhibits your advance as a church, and without a doubt, it inhibits your advance as a follower of Jesus. If you don't believe me, ask the apostle Peter. The scene for the conversation is the shore of the Sea of Galilee. Peter has been through the agony of denying he knew Jesus at His death, the emotions of seeing Him alive again, and most recently a restoration conversation on the beach. At the tail end of that conversation, after Jesus has just told Peter the kind of death he was going to die,

> *He said to Him, "Follow Me." Then Peter, turning around, saw the disciple whom Jesus loved following, who also had leaned on His breast at*

> *the supper, and said, "Lord, who is the one who*
> *betrays You?" Peter seeing him, said to Jesus,*
> *"But Lord, what about this man?" Jesus said to*
> *him, "If I will that he remain till I come, what is*
> *that to you? You follow Me."*
> *John 21:19–22*

Jesus was trying to let Peter know, in no uncertain terms, that comparison will paralyze your ability to advance as a follower. Peter was just told by Jesus that He was going to die for Him, and Peter must have thought, "Maybe so, but somebody better be killing John too. I mean, if I have to die for Jesus, then so should he." Comparison. Just imagine if Jesus would have let that comment go. Peter could have harbored resentment and bitterness toward John, and maybe even toward Jesus, that would have crippled him in following Jesus. But Jesus didn't let his comments go. Simply put, Jesus told Peter it was none of his business what He wanted John to do. Peter's business was to follow Jesus. Period.

Wouldn't it be great if that message actually saturated our hearts to the point that we could get past comparison? The rub of the whole matter of comparison is that there is always somebody better than you or another church or company doing a better job than yours. But the attraction outweighs the rub because there is always somebody worse too—always another person or company or church not doing as well. That is why comparison is so destructive. It engages you in this vicious, never-ending cycle, which forces you to look around so much that you cannot advance. Your eyes are very active but you aren't making any progress.

Imagine how the denominational gatherings would change if comparison were eliminated—if we didn't foster it by printing the "Top Ten Churches" in this category and that, but instead began to see the standard of Jesus more clearly; if you didn't have to worry about whether your church was tops in budgets or baptisms or buildings; if we didn't compare our particular denomination (or non) to every other denomination to determine our success or failure. What if we heard Jesus' voice clearly in our churches and our personal lives, "You follow Me"? We run out of excuses in light of those words, and we must make the choice to advance. Comparison kills because it causes us to look around. Leading and living as a nostalgic kills because it forces us to look back. But Jesus says "Remember." Remember what? To follow. And following requires advance.

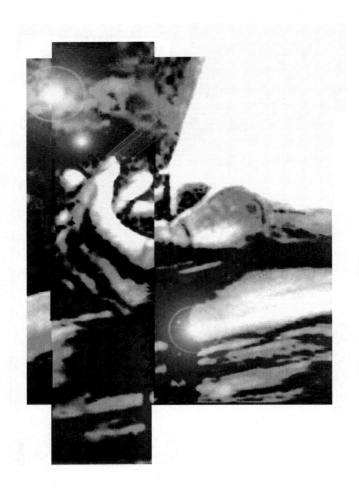

Chapter III

Authenticity

Recently, I was looking into this idea of authenticity, and I came upon some interesting websites as I was surfing the Internet. It is amazing how many sites there are that are involved with some form of "authenticity." One of note was the site of a consulting firm named Authenticity Consulting, LLC (found at www.authenticityconsulting.com). As I read about the business consulting that this firm is involved in, I noticed that they defined authenticity as "wholehearted participation in life and work." In fact, they dedicated a paragraph to the value of authenticity. Take a look at what it said,

"We strongly believe that authenticity is the most important criteria for learning in life and work. The term "authenticity" is becoming almost commonplace in literature about leadership and management development. To us, the term "authenticity" means wholehearted participation. An authentic person is someone who shows up completely and is participating as honestly as possible in the here-and-now. This authenticity is the *bottom line requirement* for any form of learning in life and work."

If you ask me, they are on to something. I think

that authenticity is the bottom line requirement for the Jesus follower as well, and I would also concur that authenticity is the only means of really learning in our spiritual journey. Why? Because authenticity is directly linked to that character trait that identifies who we are at the core of our being. In other words, authenticity is the reflection of the motives of our heart.

What Moves You?

It would be of substance to consider that the root word for "motivation" is the word "motive." Motive is that state of the heart that informs our behavior. The Bible phrases it this way, *For as he thinks in his heart, so is he* (Proverbs 23:7, NKJV). Motive is what yields behavior. It is our motivation to do what we do. Even when we don't really know what we believe, our actions tell us. Sure, we may have a theological structure of truths and doctrines with which we intellectually agree, but that doesn't mean that we believe them. We agree that without faith it is impossible to please God, but we often live faithless lives relying on our own ability and strength. So can we really say that we *believe* it? We agree that without knowing Jesus, people will end up in a crisis eternity, but we are not involved in outreach and missions. Is it then fair to say that we actually *believe* that? What you *believe* is what you actually *do*; the rest is just philosophy and empty talk. And what we believe comes from what moves us. If we could work toward changing what people cared about before we tried to change their beliefs, then we would actually be a step ahead in the process. Because for most people, what they are moved by is what they believe. What does this have to do with being authentic? Well, I would suggest that what you are moved by demonstrates the authentic you. The "Christian" of the western world is oftentimes frustrated and seemingly unmoved in their followship of Jesus. Why? Maybe because we are concentrating on the wrong things to motivate us.

I loved this girl ever since sixth grade (literally). She was skinny because she was a junior Olympic runner, and I was skinny because I was so picky when it came to food. I thought this was a match made in heaven. During my entire middle school career, I don't think I even had a girlfriend because I didn't want to lose my shot with this girl if I ever caught a whiff of her interest in me. I wanted to sit next to her in class if possible, be near her when I could, and always make sure that she knew that I was paying attention to her. It was like a middle school *Fatal Attraction* without the burning bunny, sharp utensils, or evil schemes (ok, maybe it was just puppy love).

As we went to high school, I still did not think anyone could measure up to her. She began dating other guys in high school, and I just remained her friend although I was holding out hope that she would finally come to her senses and see Prince Charming (that would be me). Finally, after nearly six long years of waiting, she was without a boyfriend and the Senior Prom was drawing near. I turned down one girl who asked me to take her to the prom (in part because her all-state wrestler ex-boyfriend would be capable of grinding me to dust powder if he was overcome with the jealousy bug). I had my heart set on Edie. It worked out because I got word through some secret agent work with some of our mutual friends that she would say "yes" if I asked her to the prom. I asked; she accepted. But, it was just as "friends." At that point, I didn't care if it was just as enemies, my heart wanted to be with her and nobody else.

Fast forward to college. Edie and I both attended

the University of Georgia, and my heart's desire for her had not changed one bit. But at this point, the feeling was not necessarily mutual. She was dating other people and moving ahead with her life, while I seemed to be hanging on to a pipedream. I felt empty and frustrated, so I tried dating. I figured that the emptiness and frustration were a result of not having a girlfriend. I was wrong. I dated other girls who were very beautiful and extremely nice, but I still was frustrated and empty. I could not seem to convince my heart that what I needed was a girlfriend. My heart kept telling me that I needed Edie. I knew that was the authentic me because if Edie would have made known to me that she liked me, I would have dropped every girl on the face of the earth to be with her. My actions proved to me what my heart was all about. It was all about her. Just the mention of her name would bring a visceral response from me, but I kept trying to replace her with other things in an effort to deceive my heart. It started to work; I became numb for a while, emotionless. I relied on *things* to satisfy the longings of my heart, whether they were relationships or sporting events or prideful accomplishments or any number of other things. This was just how life was, or so I thought. I had successfully killed off authenticity.

As depressing as that thought is, I am fearful that it is the state of many a "Christian." The heart is not engaged in following Jesus because we have duped ourselves into thinking that it is about things: church attendance, serving, rules, strategies, rote devotional times, etc. Or maybe we think that a relationship with someone else is what we need. All the while we have lost our true heart in the process, the one that began the journey following Jesus, not things, and the one that used to feel the adrenaline surge at the mention of His name. The true heart that was willing to go wherever He said go, do whatever He said to do, and risk whatever He said to risk. We just wanted to be around Him, to get near Him, and everything else for us was secondary. We would drop everything for Him the moment we heard His voice. Do you remember?

That is why I suggested earlier that maybe we are trying to get motivated in our followship of Jesus by the wrong things. The only motive in our true hearts that will lead us to satisfaction is a person. The Person. The One we used to know so well, maybe. For many, the pursuit of Jesus has become a race to acquire as many facts about Him as possible, yet never dialoguing with Him about those things—facts with no relationship. It's almost like a never-ending scavenger hunt. This will always leave us empty and frustrated in our experiences, and will never motivate us to a heart pounding authenticity that results in faith filled behavior, because we have said no to our true heart.

> *Nevertheless I have this against you, that you*
> *have left your first love.*
> *Revelation 2:4*

Jesus knows when we are not authentic in our desire to love Him and follow Him wholeheartedly. And we have all been there. Some are still there. But if it is true that authenticity is the bottom line requirement for learning and growing on this journey with Jesus, then we better not stay there. So, what do we do?

Remember

After Jesus expressed to the church of Ephesus

what He had against them, He also gave them a prescription to solve it.

> **Remember** *therefore from where you have fallen. (Revelation 2:5a, bold added)*

It's like I mentioned earlier, we must reflect back to that time when we walked so closely with Jesus that we could almost sense it again. We have to wipe the dust off the mind that has tried to crowd out our true self, and remember what used to be. The power of remembering is a strong force indeed. It can cause our hearts to break. It can inspire us toward change. And it can reconnect us again to our true hearts–the new hearts that God placed within us when we opened our lives to Him. But we must put our remembrance into action. That is the next part of the prescription.

Repent

> *Remember therefore from where you have fallen;* **repent** *and do the first works. (Revelation 2:5, bold added)*

We must first remember before we repent; that is part of the power of remembrance. When we recall what used to be, how we formerly followed Jesus with authenticity, then it confirms to us how far we have drifted. That is why we must repent, or turn away from the empty, frustrating life of now and ask God to bring us back to authenticity. It's not about being everything you were or looking like you used to (in other words, no need for big hair, parachute pants, etc.). It's about getting back to your true heart, the desire to love and follow Jesus that always motivated everything about you.

Repentance, which is a change of thought that leads to a change of action, is the essence of authenticity. The reason it is so closely attached to authenticity is because of its association with humility. Humility is not the absence of self-love or worse, an intentionally derogatory view of self. It is most notably the absence of pride. Pride is the mask of the actor. Humility is the removal of the mask. To be genuinely humble is to be authentic, because until we can get honest with God and others, there will be no capacity for internal change. The prescription that Jesus offers is not one to simply make us feel better. It is to alter us, to internally redesign us so that our lives and hearts are in harmony with His.

Remembrance and repentance impact the thoughts of our mind and the disposition of our hearts, but there must be action to follow. So what does Jesus suggest?

Redo

*Remember therefore from where you have fallen; repent and **do the first works**.*
(Revelation 2:5, bold added)

For those of you reading this book, who are already Jesus followers, do you remember the things you did when you first got to know Him? Do you remember pouring your heart out to Him and believing that He was not only listening, but that He was actively involved in doing something about what you shared with Him? How about when you could not wait to get to your place of service at the church because you knew God wanted to use you for His eternal purposes? Or when every conversation you had with someone was an open invitation to brag on the incredible grace and life-change that you had experienced through Jesus? Regardless of what those things were for you, my guess is that they were motivated out of a heart of faith in Jesus. The Bible tells us that this heart is to characterize who we are at all times.

> *As you therefore have received Christ Jesus the Lord, so walk in Him, rooted and established in the faith, as you have been taught, abounding in it with thanksgiving.*
> *Colossians 2:6–7*

Walking by faith means we are to completely embrace the leadership of Jesus just like we did when we first entrusted our lives to Him. That is the key to living authentically because we are living out of the true heart that Jesus has given to us. We have to get back to that place that we used to know where we loved and lived by faith in Jesus. So what holds us up? Well, like I mentioned earlier, we have looked to the wrong things to motivate us.

> *Beware lest anyone cheat you through philosophy and empty deceit, according to the tradition of men, according to the basic principles of the world, and not according to Christ.*
> *Colossians 2:8*

> *Are you so foolish? Having begun in the Spirit, are you now being made perfect by the flesh?*
> *Galatians 3:3*

To really start living authentically, we may have

to go back to the beginning and do what we used to do with the proper heart motivation. This will reconnect the follower's heart to the Leader's heart, and will enable people to see a clearer visual of the Leader's life within us.

From Beginning to End

Getting our hearts back to the bottom line requirement of authenticity is just the start. We have to go all the way with authenticity. That means that we are willing to go all the way in following Jesus, no matter what that means. I really think that Jesus not only expects authenticity, but He demands it. And I think what He counts as an authentic life would look something like this: *Loving and following Jesus regardless of the situation or its outcome.* To be honest, I don't just think this is right, I know it is. And the reason I know is because Jesus said so.

At the end of John's Gospel, we run into a confused and maybe somewhat despondent Peter. His mind is spinning with all that has happened in the last few days—the arrest and ultimate death of Jesus, Peter's own denial of Him, and the almost unbelievable news of the Lord's resurrection. So, he decides to go fishing. And being the magnetic leader that he is, some of the other disciples decide to join him. After catching nothing all night, Jesus shows up on the shore of the Sea of Galilee, and after giving them some fishing advice, the disciples caught 153 big fish in one net. Soon the disciples came to shore and ate breakfast with Jesus, and just after that, Jesus pulled Peter aside to talk to Him. Peter must have felt some shame, but Jesus didn't shame him. Jesus simply talked to him about love and its cost. He talked to him about what it meant to be authentic.

> *"Most assuredly, I say to you, when you were younger, you girded yourself and walked where you wished; but when you are old, you will stretch out your hands, and another will gird you and carry you where you do not wish." This He spoke, signifying by what death he would glorify God. And when He had spoken this, He said to him, "Follow Me."*
> *John 21:18–19*

Historians have recorded for us in antiquity some information that was not recorded in the context of Scripture. One of those occurrences is in the manner of the apostle Peter's death. We are told that Peter died by crucifixion just like Jesus, with one exception. Peter was crucified upside down because he felt he was unworthy to die in the same manner as the Lord.[4] Jesus told him that this is what was going to happen to him. And just after telling Peter how he was going to die, He made one brief, compelling statement.

"Follow Me."

It's hard for me to process what Peter was hearing from Jesus. Nobody has ever communicated to me the manner in which I was going to die, and then told me to follow them to my death. I don't know that I would want to hitch a ride on that train. He didn't tell Peter when he was going to die. Tomorrow? Next week? Next year? He didn't tell Him specifically how to prepare for it nor all of the particular events surrounding it. He only told him the way to get there, "Follow Me." Why such a hard statement?

Because following Jesus is about authenticity, and authenticity can only really be seen when we love and follow Jesus, regardless of the outcome. The good news is that Peter displayed his authenticity as a follower from that day forward. Listen to what the aged apostle writes:

> *In this you greatly rejoice, though now for a little while, if need be, you have been grieved by various trials, that the genuineness [authenticity] of your faith, being much more precious than gold that perishes, though it is tested by fire, may be found to praise, honor, and glory at the revelation of Jesus Christ.*
> *1 Peter 1:6–7 (brackets added)*

Peter got back to his true heart; the one Jesus gave him at the beginning that was motivated by a love for Him. He became an authentic follower because he finished how he started. He knew that even though the outcome for his life was going to be difficult, his heart said, "Follow."

By the way, just to give you some closure to the story I told you about the girl I loved since sixth grade, and to make sure that you didn't think that I am in ongoing counseling for depression, here is the finale. Not long after I had successfully killed off authenticity in my life, a young lady introduced me to the claims of Jesus and explained to me what the Bible said about His love for me. I embraced Jesus and my life was drastically changed. I was new: new heart, new mind. I was content to live my life in love with Jesus, even if that meant never having a dating relationship or getting married. Shortly after meeting Jesus, I found out that Edie had made the same commitment to Jesus just months before me. Some months later, she started attending a Bible study I was leading, and we became friends again. Well, we ended up being more than friends. She is my wife—not a bad ending to that story, huh?

Obviously, not every story ends with the fairy tale. Peter's certainly didn't. Maybe yours has not either. But let me take just a brief moment to remind you that there is more to the story than this life is willing to communicate. Even though Peter suffered and died, he lovingly and willingly followed Jesus in spite of the situation or its outcome. That authenticity of his relationship with Jesus paid off. You see, Peter exited this life and entered into eternity where he was reunited with His Leader, Jesus. No more pain. No more persecution. In fact, Peter got to go to a place like he never dreamed or imagined. And he gets to stay forever. Jesus even named a portion of this incomparable city after him (note Revelation 21:14). And while you may not have a part of the city named after you, it is a city that you can one day enter if you have an authentic personal relationship with Jesus, and you too can stay forever.

Not a bad ending to that story either.

Chapter IV

Mission

Every journey worth taking has a mission. As we advance on our journey, the implication is that there is a point in moving forward. We are headed somewhere, guided by purpose. We have a mission.

In the classic movie *The Blues Brothers,* Jim Belushi and Dan Ackroyd had it right. We *are* on a mission from God. But what kind of mission? Are we all to be pastors and teachers? Should each of us sail the seven seas or travel to the remotest jungles of the earth for the sake of our mission? Not necessarily, although some will. So, how do we know our mission? Well, it begins by getting acquainted with the mission of the One we follow.

Ours is a shared mission. Jesus sums up very clearly one of the key aspects of His mission to the earth as He interacts with a tax collector named Zaccheus. After the disreputable Zaccheus turns away from his life of crime and vows to restore all he has stolen (and then some), Jesus makes this statement in Luke 19:9–10:

> *And Jesus said to him, "Today salvation has come to this house, because he also is a son of Abraham; for the Son of Man has come to seek and to save that which was lost."*

That's as clear a personal mission statement as I have ever seen. And since ours is a shared mission, then we must take our cue from the mission of our Leader if we want to understand our own mission. Jesus' mission was about people: finding the lost, bringing light to the dark hearts of humanity, seeking and rescuing.

This clarity of Jesus' mission helps us understand the mission that He laid before His first followers. Take a look at the words He spoke to some fishermen named Peter and Andrew:

> *"Follow Me, and I will make*
> *you fishers of men."*
> *Matthew 4:19*

Now if you are anything like me, this passage can cause a great deal of concern for one simple reason—I hate fishing. I'm coming clean and just admitting it, and it didn't even take an appearance on Oprah or an interview with Barbara Walters to get it out of me. I just don't like fishing. I know, having grown up in Georgia that I should have developed some affinity for bass and trout, and you might also assume that I know a thing or two about hunting deer as well. You would be woefully wrong. I don't own a shotgun, bow and arrow, or a slingshot. I don't drive a truck that can get me out of a mud bog. I don't know the points leader in NASCAR, or the names of all the Confederate generals in the Civil War, or watch reruns of The Dukes of Hazard. And I don't like fishing (but make no mistake, I do like grits).

Before you assume that I am stating my dislike of fishing before ever having tried it, you must know that I have given fishing a reasonable effort. I actually wanted to like it, but after trying it a few times, I just could not take it. After baiting the hook with bread (I know, I know, bread sounds ridiculous but that's what my fishing partners told me to use), I then commenced to sit in the same spot for roughly four decades without so much as a nibble. So I moved to a different location with the same result, and then another and another. You get the picture. I finally had to quit (in part because I had wasted so much time that I wanted to go to the post office and pick up the backlog of Social Security checks waiting on me). Doing nothing for hours on end should not be called fishing. In fact, it already has a name. Sleep. What I will admit, however, is that one of the times I was fishing, I did catch a fish, and it was pretty exciting. It's the process that I just can't live with. So what is someone like me to do with Jesus' statement about being a "fisher of men?" Are those of us that are non-fishermen destined to miss our mission? I think the only reason you and I might miss our mission is if we miss Jesus' point.

One of the keys to understanding what Jesus said is to understand the context of the event. Jesus was speaking to fishermen, and as a result, he used a metaphor describing their mission that was appropriate to their context. Where we miss the point today is by taking the metaphor "fishers of men" and elevating it above the mission. I think it is important to note that the Bible does not record any of the other earliest disciples of Jesus being told they would be fishers of men. He didn't say that to Matthew (Levi). He told Matthew, the tax collector, to simply, "Follow Me" (note Mark 2:14). He also said the same thing to Philip (John 1:43). To the well read Nathanael, who was reclining under a fig tree, Jesus took a different approach that was appropriate to the person and the context. So, of all the records that the Bible gives us concerning the call of Jesus' first disciples, there are only a few people whom

Jesus says He will make fishers of men. And they were all fishermen. Why is that, and what does that mean to our mission?

My best take on the whole matter is to simplify it and think back to the time of Jesus for a moment. It seems obvious that there is no way that Andrew and Peter knew the full implication of what Jesus was saying to them when He told them they would be fishers of men. But what Jesus knew was that fishing was very dear to their hearts, and it was something they were very skilled at doing. So Jesus put their mission (to reach out to people with the news of the Savior) in a metaphor that inspired them and that they could understand. I really think this communicates two things we all need to hear: we have the same mission with unique roles.

UNIQUE ROLE

Your role and mine in the Great Mission is not crafted from a cookie cutter. We are not all fishermen. Some of us are construction workers, others may be doctors, and still others are artists and musicians. We have been designed by God in very unique ways to be used in very unique roles in the Great Mission. I think that is part of what Jesus was communicating to Peter and Andrew when he told them that they would fish for men from now on. It was as if Jesus was letting them know that He really understood how they were made up, what made them tick, what their passions were, and He was going to use those things in the Great Mission of reaching people with the life altering news of salvation in Him. It is in this personal approach that Jesus takes with calling His followers that purpose, in part, finds its flame.

How has God wired you? What is your inherent

spiritual DNA that He wants to use to accomplish your personal mission within the context of the Great Mission? For Peter and Andrew, Jesus used the fishing metaphor. But what about you? Are you a construction worker? Maybe Jesus would say to you, "Follow Me, and I will make you a builder of men." You're a doctor you say? Jesus might tell you "Follow Me, and I will make you a physician of the soul." How about an artist? "Follow Me, and I will make you paint on the canvas of the heart." What about a musician? "Follow Me, and I will make you play the rhythm of God on the hearts of people."

Do you see it? Your role is unique. You were carefully crafted by the Leader to fulfill a part in this Great Mission that only you were designed to do. What energy that gives. What purpose that ignites. And what confidence that brings in the mission that our Great Leader has modeled and asked us to embrace. You don't have to be what you are not. Just be who God designed you to be, so that you can accomplish what He designed you to do. We are not all pastors or secretaries or construction workers or fishermen. But we all do have a part if we are a follower, a role perfectly suited to God's design.

SAME MISSION

While on one hand we talk about the uniqueness of our roles, the other hand is reflective of the commonality of the mission. Jesus used metaphor to ignite His followers to embrace their unique roles, but the mission in the metaphor is inescapable. The mission is about people. Whether you are fishing for men, painting on the canvas of the heart, or causing people to dance to the rhythm of God, the desired end is the same - people following Jesus. That's the point.

Jesus makes this Great Mission crystal clear for us in the gospel of Matthew:

"Go therefore and make disciples of all the nations, baptizing them in the name of the Father and of the Son and of the Holy Spirit, teaching them to observe all things that I have commanded you; and lo, I am with you always, even to the end of the age." Amen.
Matthew 28:19–20

While the primary subject of this mission statement is God (both stated and implied), the primary object of the statement is people. In fact, Jesus doesn't say just *some* people need to be disciples, but states that our mission is to *all the nations*. The Greek word translated "nations" that is used in this passage is the word from which we derive the English word "ethnic." In other words, this mission for people is not limited in its scope. We are to reach out to every ethnicity that exists so that we can see them become disciples or followers of Jesus.

One of the inspiring things about being a follower who is tapped into the Great Mission is the sense of unity we feel with all the followers of Jesus in any age. My mission and the Apostle Peter's mission are the same. We will accomplish our personal missions in different ways according to how our Leader designed us, but Peter and I are reading from the same playbook in the big scheme of things. That ignites something in me. Are there other followers who have gone before you that inspire you, maybe Martin Luther or Stephen the martyr or Mary the mother of Jesus? Or maybe it's more recent followers like Billy Graham or Corrie Ten Boom. Whoever they may be, you have something great in common with them. You follow the same Leader, and you share the same Great Mission.

The truth is we need some inspiration while carrying out the Great Mission because sometimes it seems a little dangerous. Sometimes it feels like our efforts are sabotaged and our plans are thwarted. Sometimes it feels like there is direct opposition. Sometimes it feels like we have . . . an enemy. We do.

> *Be sober, be vigilant; because your adversary*
> *the devil walks about like a roaring lion, seek-*
> *ing whom he may devour.*
> *1 Peter 5:8*

I just recently returned from spending two weeks in South Africa. I spent the first week in that great country working with a church about 70 miles from Johannesburg. During week two I was involved in preaching and teaching about 400 African pastors at a Pastors Conference in Johannesburg. After the first week of intense ministry (I preached fifteen times in 5 days at a variety of locations: hospitals, factories, schools, manure storage facilities, etc.), I was ready for a day of rest. Fortunately, our hosts had arranged for us to visit a wild game park so that we could rest and enjoy the country's native beauty before we went to teach at the Pastors Conference.

The sights were incredible. Giraffe, antelope, rhinos, hyenas, zebra, and elephants were just a few of the animals we observed from our open vehicle. The terrain was gorgeous. But all the while in the back of my mind, there was really only one animal I felt like I absolutely wanted to see. You guessed it, the lion.

We had traveled around the better part of the late afternoon, and the dark had come upon us. I thought we would not get to see a lion since it was dark, but I held out a little hope since the vehicle did have a large spotlight on it. As we were parked in one location watching a herd of about 50 elephants cross the road in front of us, we heard the roar of a lion echo off the canopy of stars in the South African sky. Our tour guide began moving in that direction, and after being told by way of radio that there were some lions sighted up the road, we finally came to that location. After searching with the spotlight for a moment, sure enough, there were three lions less than 100 yards from the road.

As we watched them, they watched us. It was kind of mesmerizing. Their red eyes (because of the spotlight) just glared at us. They did not seem very intimidated at being so close to the road. Someone asked our tour guide where the lions like to hang out. I still remember what he said. "Near the road, but out of sight." He went on to tell us that lions typically would sneak up on their prey, but they liked being near the road because they could see what was going on. They would position themselves for an attack just off the road.

So does our enemy. In the journey that we are on with Jesus, you can rest assured that the enemy is positioned just off road in an unseen position waiting for an opportunity to attack. He is trying to divert us from our mission. Maybe he is roaring to invoke fear in us, or rustling the bushes so that we take our eyes off our Leader, or leaving carcasses nearby to make us reconsider our commitment to the mission.

But we are not alone. Because ours is a common mission, we have both unity of purpose and unity of struggle with all the other followers of Jesus in the world. Note what Peter tells us after reminding us that we have a real enemy:

*Resist him, steadfast in the faith, knowing that
the same sufferings are experienced by your
brotherhood in the world.
1 Peter 5:9*

And I think that Jesus, knowing what was to come for all those who would follow Him, included a phrase of unity and comfort in His Great Mission statement. He said that He would always be with us, even to the end of the age (Matthew 28:20). Not only do we go through our trials with other followers, but Jesus promises that He will be with us too. That, in and of itself, can give us some much needed courage. The fact that our Leader Jesus put Himself in harm's way for the sake of people should convince us that the rescue mission for people is worth the risk involved.

Those that are fulfilling the mission in South Africa are seeing the wrath of the enemy displayed. They see the risk, but they value the mission for people as greater. I have seen the damage of the enemy in this territory first hand: broken lives, broken governmental structures, and broken schools. AIDS has moved past epidemic to commonplace with nearly half of the entire population of the country having HIV. Hunger, joblessness and despair are rampant, but hope yet remains.

We must remember that our enemy and our Leader are not two equal and opposite forces. This is not just the simple scenario of good versus evil where we merely hope that good will somehow win the day. This is God versus evil, and the Bible reminds us as followers:

*You are of God, little children, and have over-
come them, because He who is in you is greater
than he who is in the world.
1 John 4:4*

That's why I could stand up in front of tuberculosis patients in a South African hospital (85% of which have AIDS and will die from TB within the year), and tell them that the best is yet to come if they become followers of Jesus. Even though the enemy had persuaded them to make different choices up to this point, the greater power of God allowed them to make the choice to trust Jesus. That choice was made possible because Jesus valued the mission for people above the risks associated with rescuing them. So must we.

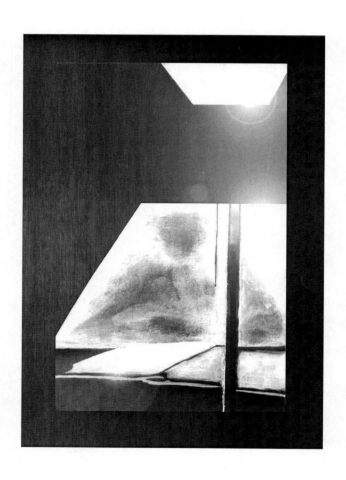

Chapter V

Trust

Running on a treadmill may very well be the cause of some forms of clinical insanity. Believe me; I am well acquainted with it (the treadmill, not insanity as yet). Because I live in Buffalo, which doesn't bode well for outdoor runners in the winter, I run on a treadmill about four months out of the year. The treadmill is not at a gym; it's in my house. The way I have it positioned is facing a wall of exposed insulation in my unfinished basement. No television in front of me, no magazines on the treadmill, just some white plastic covering the insulation staring at me. The sound of it might just drive you to go and purchase a Richard Simmons video.

To be honest, I position my treadmill that way on purpose (some line of semi-logic that tells me I will be more mentally tough when I do the triathlon for which I am training). It's something different that nearly makes me go crazy. I will run anywhere between four and five miles at one time, usually four times a week, and I will run at a relatively swift pace (notice I used the word "relatively"). My problem is that when I am finished running, I have not gone anywhere. I am in exactly the same place I was when I started. I mean, I am sweating like a church member at offering time and have nothing to show for it. I can't tell you all that I saw on my run because the scenery never changed, not even once. It's like sitting in a parked car in your garage for seven hours and telling people you took a road trip. No wonder it can make you crazy.

Well, for those of you that are frustrated and confused in your efforts to follow Jesus, I would pose this question, "Does your scenery ever change?" Now I am not suggesting that you need to relocate your home, change your job, or plant a garden in your backyard. What I am hinting at is your spiritual scenery. Do you see with different eyes than you did a year ago, two years ago, or a decade ago? Or have you been lulled to sleep by convincing yourself that you know what you need to know and you have done what you need to do spiritually? It is a dangerous place to be, and it results in ineffectiveness in the Kingdom alongside personal frustration or even boredom. Why do I even bring this up? Because it is impossible for someone whose spiritual scenery never changes to please God.

But without faith it is impossible to please Him,
for he who comes to God must believe that He
is, and that He is a rewarder of those who dili-
gently seek Him.
Hebrews 11:6

When our scenery never changes, we don't have to trust God because we know right where we are and right where we are going (nowhere). But when we really begin to advance in following Jesus, when we really start moving forward, it will require trust because we will have never traveled to that place before. It is only in trusting Him that we can really please Him. So living any other way is not an option for the follower of Jesus that really wants to please the One he is following. Let's check in again with Peter and Jesus to see this more clearly.

> *Then Peter, turning around, saw the disciple whom Jesus loved following, who also had leaned on His breast at the supper, and said, "Lord, who is the one who betrays You?" Peter, seeing him, said to Jesus, "But Lord, what about this man?" Jesus said to him, "If I will that he remain till I come, what is that to you? You follow Me."*
> *John 21:20–22*

In a previous chapter, we observed Jesus teaching Peter about what it means to be an authentic follower, and the verses noted above are the follow-up to that interchange. Peter has just learned that he will die for following Jesus at an undetermined time in the future, and no doubt his concern begins to rise. Suddenly, Peter is thrust into the arena of trust and cast out of the realm of self-reliance. Quickly and categorically, Peter's spiritual scenery begins to change, and he is not familiar with the landscape or the roadmap. Fishing he can handle because he has the skill and experience to do it, but this is different, very different.

Deep Water

You might assume Peter didn't really need this lesson from Jesus that he was about to get. I mean, Jesus showed him time and again who He really was. He even gave Peter a pretty significant lesson early in His ministry about trust vs. self-reliance:

71

*So it was, as the multitude pressed about Him
to hear the word of God, that He stood by the
Lake of Gennesaret, and saw two boats standing by the lake; but the fishermen had gone
from them and were washing their nets. Then
He got into one of the boats, which was Simon's
and asked him to put out a little from the land.
And He sat down and taught the multitudes
from the boat. When He had stopped speaking,
He said to Simon, "Launch out into the deep
and let down your nets for a catch." But Simon
answered and said to Him, "Master, we have
toiled all night and caught nothing; neverthe-
less at Your word I will let down the net." And
when they had done this, they caught a great
number of fish, and their net was breaking. So
they signaled to their partners in the other boat
to came and help them. And they came and
filled both the boats, so that they began to sink.
When Simon Peter saw it, he fell down at Jesus'
knees, saying, "Depart from me, for I am a sinful man, O Lord!" For he and all who were with
him were astonished at the catch of fish which
they had taken; and so also were James and
John, the sons of Zebedee, who were partners
with Simon. And Jesus said to Simon, "Do not
be afraid. From now on you will catch men."
So when they had brought their boats to land,
they forsook all and followed Him.*
Luke 5:1–11

While Peter might have been the professional
fisherman, and Jesus a carpenter by trade, it was clear
from the outset of their relationship who knew more about

fishing. This must have struck Peter as odd, for Jesus to assume to tell him what to do to catch fish. In fact, Peter had been out all night and caught nothing and now Jesus tells him to launch out into the deep. Any fisherman knew that the best time for catching fish in the Sea of Galilee was when the sun was not up and the best place to catch fish was in the more shallow water. So Jesus the carpenter gives Peter the fisherman a command to do exactly the opposite. Why? Because Jesus, among other things, was about to teach Peter a lesson about trust, and trust is only learned in the deep.

Sink or Swim

Swimming in the shallow end of a pool is really somewhat of a misleading thing. You are not really swimming when you are in the shallow end. You may be lounging, or bobbing, or standing, but you are not really swimming. Why would you want to swim when you can stand? Yet if we get in a pool, even in the shallow end for the entirety of the time, we say we are swimming. But we aren't. I vote that we re-name what we do in the shallow end: liquid lounging, aquatic standing, or hydro relaxation—anything but swimming.

I can watch my children and tell the difference. My oldest son began swimming lessons at the age of five. He had fun in the shallow end: going under for a moment and then jumping up to breathe, splashing his friends, and making bubbles. Then the lifeguard blew the whistle and told them to come down to the deep end. His disposition drastically changed. The bubbly, free spirited boy of eight seconds ago was now all business. This was, after all, the *deep* end.

The lifeguard asked him to jump off the side and

swim out to her. He was not so sure, but he did it. When he finally made it back to the side, you should have seen his face. His eyes were lit up like a Christmas tree, and his expression was one of absolute amazement. You see, I think he realized something in that moment. He realized that blowing bubbles and splashing his friends in the shallow end was pretty fun, but this deep end thing—this was really living.

I wonder how many people have really grasped this from the perspective of following Jesus. I wonder how many of us think that we are in the deep water of faith and trust when in truth, we are standing in the shallow water of self-reliance. We are comfortable there because we can get our face wet once in a while, enjoy the warmth of the water, and we always have friends there to splash. But there is a major problem. Anybody can do that. Anybody can stay in the shallow end. The problem is that you don't need Jesus in the shallow end.

Ask yourself whether or not there are areas of your life where you are demonstrating complete trust in Jesus, areas where you are by faith way over your head. Or maybe you are still relying on your own ability to understand, rationalize, quantify or justify. You want to trust God with a minimum of giving ten percent of your pay to Kingdom work, but it just doesn't make financial sense to you. You want your kids to learn to love Jesus, but you rationalize that you are not qualified to teach them. So it is the job of the educators at the church. You "believe" that the whole world needs to know Jesus, but you will never launch out and actually tell someone about His love for them. This is life in the shallow end. Better stated, this is *existence* in the shallow end. You are only really living when you are in the deep end.

Crisis of Trust

Now there is always a critical time period when we are asked to go to the spiritual deep. Maybe the term crisis might apply more ably. I think the crisis we find ourselves with in the deep end is not so much the fear of not being able to sustain ourselves. Clearly, that is a valid concern people have, and no doubt it has kept people from ever entering the water in the first place. But I think the real crisis comes for us when we get in the deep end and realize that although we are not swimming on our own anymore, our heads are still above water. We begin to get a glimpse of the power that Jesus has, and for many, this is where the crisis begins. I know what you may be thinking. "Jerry, this isn't a crisis, this is great. Jesus demonstrates his power and his faithfulness to us - how can it get better than that?" I agree temporarily. At the moment that Jesus shows His faithfulness to us in the deep water of faith, it is the best thing in the world. It is after that when the crisis comes, because we begin to realize that He is going to ask us to do it again, and again, and again. Have you ever heard someone say, speaking of completing some incredible accomplishment, "That was the coolest thing I have ever done, but I never want to do it again?" I am suggesting that very thought process is the crisis. I know I have experienced it before. And I think Peter the fisherman did too.

After Jesus tells Peter to launch out into the deep and let down his nets, the incredible happens. They catch so many fish that the weight of the fish is actually causing the boats to take on water. This had to be a Sea of Galilee fishing record. Peter's name would be in large print on a plaque at the Yacht Club. The *Jerusalem Post* would do a full-page layout. He would never have to lie about a fish story for the rest of his life. But instead of jumping up and down and celebrating, Peter responds to Jesus in a somewhat peculiar manner. He says to Jesus, "Depart from me, for I am a sinful man, O Lord!"

I have heard the explanations on this statement of Peter just like you have. Most of them suggest, in one way or another, that Peter was humbled by the greatness of Jesus, and upon that realization he confessed his own unworthiness to be in His presence. In other words, this was a statement of Peter's deep piety and spiritual awareness. Well, in the words of *ESPN College Game Day's* Lee Corso, "not so fast my friend." I think there is more here than meets the eye. I think Peter was facing a crisis of trust.[5]

If Peter was so awed at the power of Jesus, then why didn't He respond in the same way just a few days earlier when Jesus was at his house healing the sick and casting out demons (Luke 4:38–41)? If I were given the choice of seeing tons of fish or demons getting kicked out of people, I would go with the demon bashing every time. Peter saw this, but he didn't respond like he did when he caught all the fish. Why was that? Maybe because Peter realized that this was the way Jesus wanted life lived, and Peter would have to give up what he could handle on his own to live like that.

Peter was scared. Jesus confirmed that he was scared by saying to him, "Do not be afraid." I would have been scared too. If I had just hit the mother load like Peter, and was being asked to leave it behind for an uncertain future with a man I did not even know that well, you better believe I would be nervous. But I don't think Peter's major crisis was between leaving and staying. I think it was between controlling and trusting. With that catch of fish, Peter could have bought a bigger boat to increase the business. He could have put a little nest egg away for retirement, and maybe even taken his family on a vacation to the Dead Sea Magic Kingdom. He could have control, so to speak, over his own destiny, or at the very least been a few legs up. But Jesus asked Peter to trust Him, and Jesus would reiterate that theme over and over again.

Back to the Future

Back to Jesus and Peter after the resurrection, as recorded in the twenty first chapter of John's gospel:

> *Peter seeing him [John], said to Jesus, "But Lord, what about this man?" Jesus said to him, "If I will that he remain till I come, what is that to you? You follow Me." (Emphasis mine)*

This passage teaches a very important truth about trust. It shows us that trust is personal. As simple as that sounds, I think that it often gets lost in real life. We are all too willing to trust Jesus corporately when we are moving forward by faith in an area of church life. Maybe it's a particular outreach program, or building a new facility, or something that serves the community, and we find ourselves in favor of it from a corporate perspective. But if we are asked to be involved personally, then we are less enthusiastic and may even question whether or not it is the right thing to do.

What I am saying is that we want an easy way of following Jesus so we design our own plan. That plan looks something like this: We want a *personal relationship* with Jesus but we only want to embrace a *corporate followship.* But with Jesus, it does not work that way. Peter tested Him on it. He asked Jesus what was going to happen to John. I can hear him now, "Jesus, if I have to die for following you, then doesn't John? I mean, if you recall that time you were out on the water and called to us, I came walking out on the water. And where was John? Sitting in the boat. Remember the garden, when the soldiers came to take you away and I cut off Malchus' ear to help protect you? Where was John? Running away into the night. So surely if I have to die for you, he will too, won't he? What is going to happen to him?" Peter wanted to remove himself from the personal responsibility of following Jesus, at least in following Him alone.

Jesus deals with this question in as straight forward a manner as possible. He says, in my paraphrase, "Peter, it is none of your business what I do with John. I want you to follow Me regardless of what anyone else is doing." You see, if Jesus gives us the privilege of a personal relationship with Him, then attached to that is the responsibility of a personal followship as well. You can't get out of it. It is part of the deal.

There are going to be times in our lives that the road in following Jesus is crowded. Those are the fun times. Your friends are making choices to obey and follow Jesus in certain areas of their lives, and it feels as if you can travel in the journey together as followers. But there will be other times when the road seems to be empty. It's just you and Jesus. There are occasions where these times are not as easy or enjoyable. You will have to initiate the reconciliation of a relationship, even though you did nothing wrong. You will not be able to talk a certain way to people anymore, even though it seems as if everyone else can get by with it. You may be called on to sacrifice some material things for the sake of Jesus' cause while others are stockpiling. You may even be called upon to carry the gospel to places that nobody else will go. Whether the road of obedience is crowded or empty, one thing remains sure. Jesus has given us the responsibility of personally following Him—trusting Him, regardless of what anyone else in the entire world is doing. The hymn writer of days gone by got it right, "Though none go with me, I still will follow, no turning back, no turning back." It's personal. It's deep, and it goes way beyond our capacity for self-reliance. It's trust.

Chapter VI

Courage

It's no secret that I think *Braveheart* is one of the great movies of all time. Maybe it's a man thing, but there is something about the lead character, William Wallace, that resonates with me. I don't intend to imply that he reminds me of myself. I am not really strong, and I don't look particularly desirable in a kilt. I think what most captures me is his courage. Maybe it's because I see the value of that virtue, or because it takes me to a place in my heart that I know exists yet have a hard time accessing. Either way, courage strikes a chord on the strings of my soul.

The nobility of courage is somewhat hard to define. We know it when we see it, and we also know it when we feel it, but sometimes it is hard to put into words. While I know that I cannot capture courage with a simple definition, I do want to offer you an understanding of what I mean when I refer to it.

Courage is that virtue that knows that although faith and fear co-exist, faith must ultimately win the day.

I realize that a first reading of this understanding of courage may cut against what you believe to be true.

I have both heard it taught and probably taught it myself that faith and fear cannot co-exist. They are polar opposites. Where there is fear, there cannot be faith, and where there is faith, there can be no fear. In theory, that sounds like truth. The funny thing about theories, though, is that they need to be tested to prove true. Without a doubt, this theory fails the test. Anyone who has ever taken a real step of faith knows that it is scary. You do not have control anymore; you have yielded it to someone else. That is, and always will be, frightening. That is why we need courage.

If you do not walk by faith, then you really do not need courage. There is a sense of comfort in plotting our own course and controlling our own destiny. You don't need courage for that. But try living by faith and making some decisions that reflect you are living by faith, and then you will lose all sense of comfort and control. You will need courage. In our journey with Jesus, I believe that the virtue of courage is designed for the follower that is willing to take steps of faith. You see, courage is connected to both faith and fear. To walk by faith requires courage. To overcome fear requires courage. That is why courage is so necessary, because faith and fear co-exist. The nobility of courage knows that although faith and fear co-exist, it is imperative that faith wins the day.

Urban Courage

James Galliard is a friend of mine. From the moment I met him, I realized that there was something special about this man. We met on a flight from Atlanta to South Africa that covered fifteen hours. For almost the entire duration of the flight down, we just talked about all that God was up to in our lives and ministries. James told me that this was really his first ministry experience on foreign soil. He even admitted he was a little pensive about the whole thing. Well, since I was a veteran of foreign travel and mission trip opportunities all over the world, I thought to myself that I could provide him with some additional courage on this journey. At least I thought that until I heard the story of what God is using him to do. Then I made sure that I kept my mouth shut.

James, an articulate, educated man, was enjoying professional success in the corporate sector. He was making a very substantial salary by anyone's standards, and had the personal effects to prove it. As a Jesus follower, James sensed that God wanted more from him. In fact, he sensed that God wanted all of him. Having grown up in Philadelphia, James was compelled by a deep desire to make an impact in his city that was fueled by the message of hope in Jesus Christ, but he knew that God didn't want him in the suburbs. God wanted James in the heart of a city with incredibly deep needs. So, he planted a church in a very depressed area of Southwest Philly, but he didn't just plant his church there. He planted his family there as well. He left his large salary and traded it for very little. In fact, the average annual per capita income for residents of his neighborhood is $11,640 a year. He began the church in June of 2000 with 23 people in a dilapidated building that was 100 years old. There were pigeons flying through the building during the service, no bathrooms, no heating system, no sound system, no musical instruments, no finances, drug dealers on the corner, and prostitutes on the church steps. Although faith was at the core of what James was doing, it was clear that fear was making its presence known as well.

But courage knew that faith must win the day, and did it ever. Word Tabernacle Baptist Church is now one of the fastest growing ministries in the country. This church is now planting other churches. In fact, James has sensed God's call to plant a church in the urban section of Rocky Mount, North Carolina as well. And at the time of this writing, he is pastoring two churches at the same time (one of the church plants in Philadelphia, and the new church plant in Rocky Mount). If that were not enough to keep him busy, James has also initiated The Urban Sanctuary, an organization that partners with various political, social, and religious entities for the purpose of renewing the urban culture. Because of James's courage, Southwest Philadelphia, Rocky Mount, North Carolina, and many other urban communities are being transformed.

Fear Factor

Even the best men and women face fear. They always have, even as far back as 3400 years ago. During that period, a man by the name of Joshua was taking the reigns of leadership over Israel from his famous predecessor Moses. Moses was an iconic figure. He seemed larger than life. Yet God had let Joshua know that since Moses was dead, He wanted him to take over and lead the people of Israel into the promised land of Canaan. This had to be intimidating for Joshua. He had watched as Moses confronted Egypt's Pharaoh, saw his rod turn into a snake, saw the Red Sea part at his command, and observed the commandments that God had carved out on stone and delivered to him. Joshua must have thought to himself that filling the shoes of Moses was nearly impossible, not to mention assuming the leadership of hundreds of thousands of people. It had to be scary.

It was scary, and God knew it too. Notice what he says to Joshua:

"Be strong and of good courage, for to this
people you shall divide as an inheritance the
land which I swore to their fathers to give them.
Only be strong and very courageous ... ...
... ... Have I not commanded you?
Be strong and of good courage; do not be
afraid, nor be dismayed, for the Lord your God
is with you wherever you go."
Joshua 1:6–7a, 9 (emphasis mine)

Joshua was brave. He had proven that over forty years earlier when he spied out the land and reported back to Moses that it was there for the taking. But even Joshua needed courage now. The price tag of his faith was in facing up to the fear associated with faith. It's no wonder that God so emphasized to him the need for courage. God graces us with the virtue of courage because He knows that we cannot fulfill His purpose of walking by faith without it.

I identify with Joshua. Now, I'm not saying that I am like him. I would hope to be half the man that he was. But I understand, even if only in part, some of the challenges he faced. In coming to pastor The Chapel in Buffalo, New York, I was walking into my first position as lead pastor. I had served in full time ministry for a decade, but this was my first opportunity to be the leader. The founding pastor of the church, who died just a few years before my coming, was somewhat of an iconic figure in Buffalo. He led the church for nearly forty years, had a television broadcast, and was somewhat of a larger than life figure to many people. The pastor who took over for him after his death was committed to transitioning to a younger leader for the future. But to make matters worse, the present pastor was over thirty years my senior, had been in ministry for roughly forty years, and had a track record of faithful, successful, God blessed service—not just one tough act to follow, but two. Great. Thanks a lot.

Needless to say, I was a bit intimidated at God's call to lead this church, even though I was positive that it was His direction. But just because I was sure that I heard God's voice to come to Buffalo, it did not eliminate the fear associated with that decision. That was true of Joshua as well. He heard the voice of God. In fact, he heard the audible voice of God telling him to lead Israel across the Jordan River into the Promised Land. But that didn't eliminate all fear because even as God was giving him his marching orders, He was also telling him to have courage.

As I write, I stand in need of courage. God has really been active in our faith community, and as a result, we are in the process of relocating our entire campus to a different location to position ourselves for the future. But it is a scary endeavor. There are occasions when I think to myself that I have helped to lead all of these great people off a cliff. Not only are we re-positioning a campus that has a storied history, but we are even adjusting the name of the church when we arrive at our new location. We have changed the look and function of the staff. We have made significant changes in philosophy and programming throughout the whole church. And now, on top of that, we are asking the people to give millions of dollars to finance more change. Some pastors that I know have been tarred and feathered for much less. But I am reminded that it is a journey that we, as a body of believers, entered together, affirming that it is God's direction for our church. We, as a church, understand that our mission is to bring maximum glory to God and reach the most people we can for Christ.

And to do that means that we need courage because it is imperative that faith wins the day if we are to realize God's design for us.

Aqua Courage

One of the classic reminders of both fear and courage being displayed in the same event comes to us by way of Peter, one of Jesus' closest associates. You probably remember the scene. The disciples are out in a boat crossing over the Sea of Galilee. While they are in the middle of the water a nasty storm kicks up. Then Jesus comes out to them, walking on the water.

> *And when the disciples saw Him walking on the sea, they were troubled, saying, "It is a ghost!" And they cried out for fear. But immediately Jesus spoke to them, saying, "Be of good cheer [take courage]! It is I; do not be afraid." And Peter answered Him and said, "Lord, if it is You, command me to come to You on the water." So He said, "Come." And when Peter had come down out of the boat, he walked on the water to go to Jesus. But when he saw that the wind was boisterous, he was afraid; and beginning to sink he cried out, saying, "Lord, save me!"*
> *Matthew 14:26–30 (brackets added).*

Through the years, much has been said about this passage. It has been noted that Peter was the only one to have the courage to get out of the boat, even though his courage and faith were short lived. I have also heard it said that Peter shows that even a little faith can get you standing on the water. You also see in this passage faith and fear co-existing, with fear ultimately winning the day. While all of these are true, I would like to approach this passage from a slightly different angle.

One of the things this passage teaches me is that sometimes what we teach as a "principle" is actually a disservice to the truth of who God really is. Certainly not every principle is a disservice to truth. I don't mean to imply that principles are wrong. They are not. The Bible is full of principles. My only contention is when those principles are looked at in isolation instead of in the light of the volume of Scripture. I also get concerned in my own teaching that I may be guilty of miniaturizing God at times—wrongly representing who He really is, sizing Him down to fit my principle. Sometimes God has fit Himself to a principle. Other times He hasn't. Let me illustrate by weaving this into our discussion about courage and fear.

I have heard it communicated many times that the answer to our fears is found in getting closer to God and experiencing His presence. It is taught as a principle, something to which God has bound Himself. But I think it is only true in part and does not give a full picture of who God really is. Before moving on, though, I would like to note that the Bible affirms this "principle" to be true at times.

> *You will show me the path of life; In your presence is fullness of joy; At your right hand are pleasures forevermore. Psalm 16:11*

> *I will love You, O Lord, my strength. The Lord is my rock and my fortress and my deliverer; My God, my strength, in whom I will trust; My shield and the horn of my salvation, my strong-*

*hold. I will call upon the Lord, who is worthy
to be praised; So shall I be saved from my enemies. Psalm 18:1–3*

*He who dwells in the secret place of the Most
High shall abide under the shadow of the
Almighty. I will say of the Lord, "He is my ref-
uge and my fortress; My God, in Him I will
trust." Psalm 91:1–2*

Both in these passages, and certainly many others in the Bible, it is proven true that our connection to
the presence of God can eradicate fear and give peace
and courage. And if you are one to believe that faith and
fear cannot co-exist, then this is an easy "principle" to
embrace. But it is only part of the story.

I would like to offer you something to think about
that I believe is equally true. *Sometimes being in the presence of God causes more fear.* Or maybe how about stating it this way: *dwelling in God's presence may be where
you exchange one fear for another one.* To see this a little
more clearly, let's look at a few examples starting with
our friend Peter.

After reading the passage about Peter walking on
the water, can it really be concluded that Peter's nearness
to the presence of Jesus alleviated his fears? Certainly not
entirely. Peter had to be somewhat fearful being caught
in the middle of a storm. Although he probably wasn't as
panicked as some others because of his experience as a
fisherman, he nonetheless likely felt some fear. So, Jesus
comes walking on the water to them and actually creates
more fear because they think that He is a ghost. Then,
upon realizing that it is Jesus, their ghost fear is alleviated.
In fact, a surge of courage and faith comes upon Peter

because he is now with Jesus and he gets out of the boat to meet Him on the water, and it works. Peter walks on the water. Fear takes a backseat. But then, of course, Peter looks around at his unusual foundation and at the size of the waves that are roaring all around him, and he begins to sink. Fear now moves to the front seat. And where was Jesus all this time? In the same location—very near Peter. So Peter went from fear to faith and back to fear all in the presence of Jesus.

Later in Peter's life, when he was falling in and out of sleep in the garden of Gethsemane, his courage rose up again. The betrayer had brought soldiers to come and take Jesus away, but the courageous Peter would have none of it. He drew his sword and cut off the ear of one of the soldiers in an effort to defend Jesus. But after they had taken Jesus away, notice what happened to the courageous fisherman.

> *And those who had laid hold of Jesus led Him away to Caiaphas the high priest, where the scribes and the elders were assembled. But Peter followed Him at a distance to the high priest's courtyard. Matthew 26:57–58*

Now, interestingly enough, the most frightening place for Peter to be was *near* Jesus. Peter followed Him at a distance and, as you recall, would ultimately say he didn't know Him. Others in the testimony of Scripture had times when they experienced more fear in the presence of God than outside His presence. Abraham, Isaac, Jacob, Moses, Gideon, Isaiah, Jonah, Zacharias, and John the Revelator would be other examples that bore similarities to Peter's experiences. But the tide would turn again for Peter. After the resurrection and ascension of Jesus, Peter then seemed to have the courage of a lion (note his activity in the first few chapters of the book of Acts). I think that Peter's courage came from a conscious understanding of the presence of Jesus in the person of the indwelling Holy Spirit. It seems clear through all of these circumstances, though, that God cannot be contained with one principle relating to courage and fear. He can both alleviate fear and create it. Not to allow for that only paints half a picture.

Courage Modeled

Jesus certainly demonstrated for those of us that follow Him what courage was all about. In fact, He was the perfect model of courage in every situation. Faith always won the day with Jesus. Fear never triumphed. And one of the most compelling demonstrations of that was in the garden of Gethsemane. The Scriptural record gives us insight into what was happening at that time:

> *And He took with Him Peter and the two sons of Zebedee, and He began to be sorrowful and deeply distressed. Then He said to them, "My soul is exceedingly sorrowful, even to death. Stay here and watch with Me." He went a little farther and fell on His face, and prayed, saying, "O, My Father, if it is possible, let this cup pass from Me; nevertheless, not as I will, but as You will."*
> *Matthew 26:37–39*

Notice that I mentioned earlier that fear never triumphed with Jesus. But I did not say fear was not present. Although I hesitate to say it, I think fear was present with Jesus. It certainly didn't win His ultimate attention, but

91

it was still present. Facing the weight of bearing all the sins of the elect for all time, the physical brutality that was awaiting Him, and the interruption of His relationship with the Father, Jesus must have had to confront fear head-on.

The reason I think fear was present is because what He said in His prayer, and ultimately what He did in giving His life, took an extraordinary courage. As I mentioned earlier, I think you only need courage when fear is present. Although Jesus knew what had to be done, He prayed that the cup of suffering could pass from Him. It was as if Jesus acknowledged in that moment the war that rages between fear and faith. But His prayer did not end there. He deferred to the will of the Father, and that took great courage.

The reason I bring out this point about fear being present even with Jesus is because of what I think it means to God's glory. It seems to me that the more frightening and distressing and fearful the thing is that God tells us to do, the more glory is brought to Him when faith wins the day. Think about it. Trusting God when we feel nothing is really at stake is one thing. But trusting God when everything is on the line and the distress and fear is at maximum capacity—now that brings God glory. Receiving glory is God's great desire because it paints a clearer picture of who He is to the world, but bringing God glory takes courage because it will take faith to do it. Wherever faith is, fear is sure to make its presence known.

So Why All the Fuss?

Far too often I have seen fear win the day in people's lives. Why? Well, one of the reasons is because people sometimes misunderstand faith. They think and have even been taught that if they have enough faith, they can have whatever they want. They can do anything they want. They also think that fear won't enter the picture if they have enough faith. Nothing could be further from the truth, and anyone who has really been called to make some choices by faith knows it. So for someone who misunderstands faith and fear, it can be very discouraging to launch out by faith yet feel fear. This causes them to assume something must be wrong with their faith, but it may be that God just wants to get greater glory from the faith that they demonstrate in the midst of fear. It shows the world that they value Jesus above any personal concerns or distresses, which brings great glory to God. And in this unpredictable journey with Jesus, He has given them the task of bringing Him glory–a glory that can be easily seen in courageous followers.

Epilogue

I don't fancy myself an Irishman, though I do have some roots in my lineage there. At convenient times, I like to act the part even though I am many generations removed. If "Danny Boy" is playing in a restaurant or a mall store, I try to convince myself that the motherland is calling. I eat Lucky Charms cereal on occasion. I admire the tradition surrounding the Blarney Stone (but, since I am not a communicable diseases enthusiast, I would pass on kissing it). I have always wanted to find the pot of gold at the end of the rainbow. Now, it's not as if I really think that a leprechaun is going to guide me there, but in the event that I did run into one, I want to be ready.

I have always been a fan of the fantastic. A creative mind loves to run into the deep caverns of magical, undiscovered worlds and explore all that they have to offer. Even though they may be creations of another's mind, I am always bound to plunge into the world they created and experience it. Whether it is a classic struggle of good versus evil with all that entails, or a kingdom of intrigue, wisdom, and mystery, I just want to go there. But many don't want to go. Or better stated, many feel that they cannot go. I think I know why. They have to leave. Leaving the world of the fantastic and extraordinary means entering again the reality of their mundane existence. So, the letdown of leaving a fantasy world outweighs the joy of discovery that it brings. For many it is simply not worth the hangover.

We have longed all of our lives for another world— a more glorious existence. We prove it time and again with our actions. We consume movies, and to a lesser degree, books. We live online. We have Santa Claus and the Easter Bunny. We even need a tooth fairy. And I think all of these can be healthy, though I respect the freedom of others who don't want to live in that world. The reason I think they can be healthy is because they serve as a reminder. Reminders can be instruments of God that play portions of a song we love but have never heard. These reminders are not so much about the present, but about what is to come. On this point I must offer the floor to the brilliant C.S. Lewis:

"Creatures are not born with desires unless satisfaction for those desires exists. A baby feels hunger: well, there is such a thing as food. A duckling wants to swim: well, there is such a thing as water. Men feel sexual desire: well, there is such a thing as sex. If I find in myself a desire which no experience in this world can satisfy, the most probable explanation is that I was made for another world. If none of my earthly pleasures satisfy it, that does not prove that the universe is a fraud. Probably earthly pleasures were never meant to satisfy it, but only to arouse it, to suggest the real thing.

If that is so, I must take care, on the one hand, never to despise, or be unthankful for, these earthly blessings, and on the other, never to mistake them for the something else of which they are only a kind of copy, or echo, or mirage. I must keep alive in myself the desire for my true country, which I shall not find till after death; I must never let it get snowed under or turned aside; I must make it the main object of life to press on to that other country and to help others to do the same."[6]

The *other country* that Lewis mentions is heaven.

For the follower of Jesus, it is the Motherland. It calls out to us clearly and often—sometimes even loudly, particularly when we are facing difficulty. It is that place that we long to go and can't wait to see. It is the thought of that place that makes everything else in this life pale. But for the follower of Jesus, heaven does not have to wait—at least not completely. True enough, heaven is a reality that will only be experienced in full when we pack up our earthly tent and move on. But pieces of the kingdom to come are still present in this life, and there is one simple reason for that. Jesus.

Without trying to add to a cliché, Jesus really is life. He told us that He is "the way, the truth, and the life."[7] Life, whether in this temporary existence, or forever in eternity, is totally dependent on Him and in Him. So that means we can taste the life of then, right now, at least in part. The follower of Jesus doesn't have to choose between fantasy and reality. Because Jesus is Reality, we can live, to some extent, in both worlds at the same time. This is crucial for the follower of Jesus because living in both worlds allows anyone to see The Life in us. It cuts through the mundane details of this existence and creates a hunger in others to want to live in that world.

As I was driving my son to school one morning, I observed something that I had never before seen. In the partly cloudy winter sky, the sun was displaying its light in a most unusual, yet beautiful, manner. Instead of the circular radiation that one most commonly sees from the sun, it radiated as if it were in a cylinder. One of the meteorologists on the radio described it as a "sundog" (referencing the sun looking like a hotdog). That was impressive enough, but the most beautiful part was above it. There was a rainbow. This rainbow, however, was different than any other rainbow I had ever observed. While it displayed all the colors I am accustomed to seeing, it did not have an arched appearance. In other words, there was no "bow" in the rainbow. It went straight up, a vertical rainbow disappearing into the highest point in the sky.

A vertical rainbow! That is where it all came together for me. There really is a pot of gold at the end of the rainbow, and there really is a guide to get me there. Interestingly enough, the gold and the guide are one and the same.

Jesus.

Our reward and the Rewarder are the same.

Jesus.

That is why this journey is worth every challenge or distress or hardship. Because the ever- present Guide has a value that far exceeds gold in this life and the life to come. Let's listen once more to our friend, the Apostle Peter.

From this time many of his disciples turned back and no longer followed him.

"You do not want to leave too, do you?" Jesus asked the Twelve. Simon Peter answered him, "Lord, to whom shall we go? You have the words of eternal life. We believe and know that you are the Holy One of God."
(John 6: 66–69)

We have nowhere else to go. Nobody else is worth following. Lead on Great Leader. Lead on.

End Notes

[1] I heard Ray Bakke speak at a Leadership Network Conference in Dallas, Texas in 2003.

[2] As quoted by his widow, Elisabeth Eliot, in her book, *Shadow of the Almighty*.

[3] I heard Erwin McManus speak at a Leadership Network Conference in Dallas, Texas in 2003.

[4] Early church tradition has always held that Peter died by crucifixion, and the writings of historian Flavius Josephus have also given insight into this event. Josephus was a contemporary of Peter.

[5] I must give thanks to author Mark Buchanan, who, in his book *Your God is Too Safe*, either directly or indirectly spawned some of the thoughts I present here.

[6] Quoted from C.S. Lewis in his incomparable classic, *Mere Christianity*.

[7] The Gospel of John, chapter 14, verse 6.

Contact Jerry Gillis
Email pastorjerry@thechapel.com

or order more copies of this book at

TATE PUBLISHING, LLC

127 East Trade Center Terrace
Mustang, Oklahoma 73064

(888) 361 - 9473

Tate Publishing, LLC

www.tatepublishing.com